I0619919

Hispanic Adventures

Aventuras Hispanas

Coloring and Activity Book
Libro de colorear y actividades

Color Hispanic culture and learn Spanish with our mascot Paco in this educational coloring book. Authentic illustrations and hands-on activities offer new perspectives on culture, fostering a community of better global citizens.

Hispanic Adventures

Aventuras Hispanas

Coloring and Activity Book
Libro de colorear y actividades

Illustrator: Paola Flores
Creative Director: Alexia Salazar
Author: Shaiska Malca

©Pura Vida Talk LLC 2023.
Published by Pura Vida Talk LLC.
ISBN: 979-8-218-31689-1

All rights reserved. No part of this publication may be reproduced, stored in a retrieval system, or transmitted in any way or any means, electronic, mechanical, photocopying, recording or otherwise, without the written permission of Pura Vida Talk LLC. For more information regarding permission write to Pura Vida Talk LLC.
www.puravidatalk.com

PURA VIDA Talk

©Pura Vida Talk. All rights reserved.

Colorea la cultura hispana y aprende inglés con Paco en este libro educativo. Ilustraciones auténticas y actividades prácticas brindan nuevas perspectivas culturales, fomentando una comunidad de mejores ciudadanos globales.

Hispanic Adventures

Aventuras Hispanas

Coloring and Activity Book
Libro de colorear y actividades

Illustradora: Paola Flores
Directora Creativa: Alexia Salazar
Autora: Shaiska Malca

©Pura Vida Talk LLC 2023.
Publicado por Pura Vida Talk LLC.
ISBN: 979-8-218-31689-1

Todos los derechos reservados. Queda prohibida la reproducción total o parcial de esta publicación, el almacenamiento en un sistema de recuperación o la transmisión de cualquier forma o medio electrónico mecánico, fotocopiado, grabación u otro, sin el permiso por escrito de Pura Vida Talk LLC. Para obtener más información sobre los permisos, escriba a Pura Vida Talk LLC.
www.puravidatalk.com

PURA VIDA TALK

©Pura Vida Talk. All rights reserved.

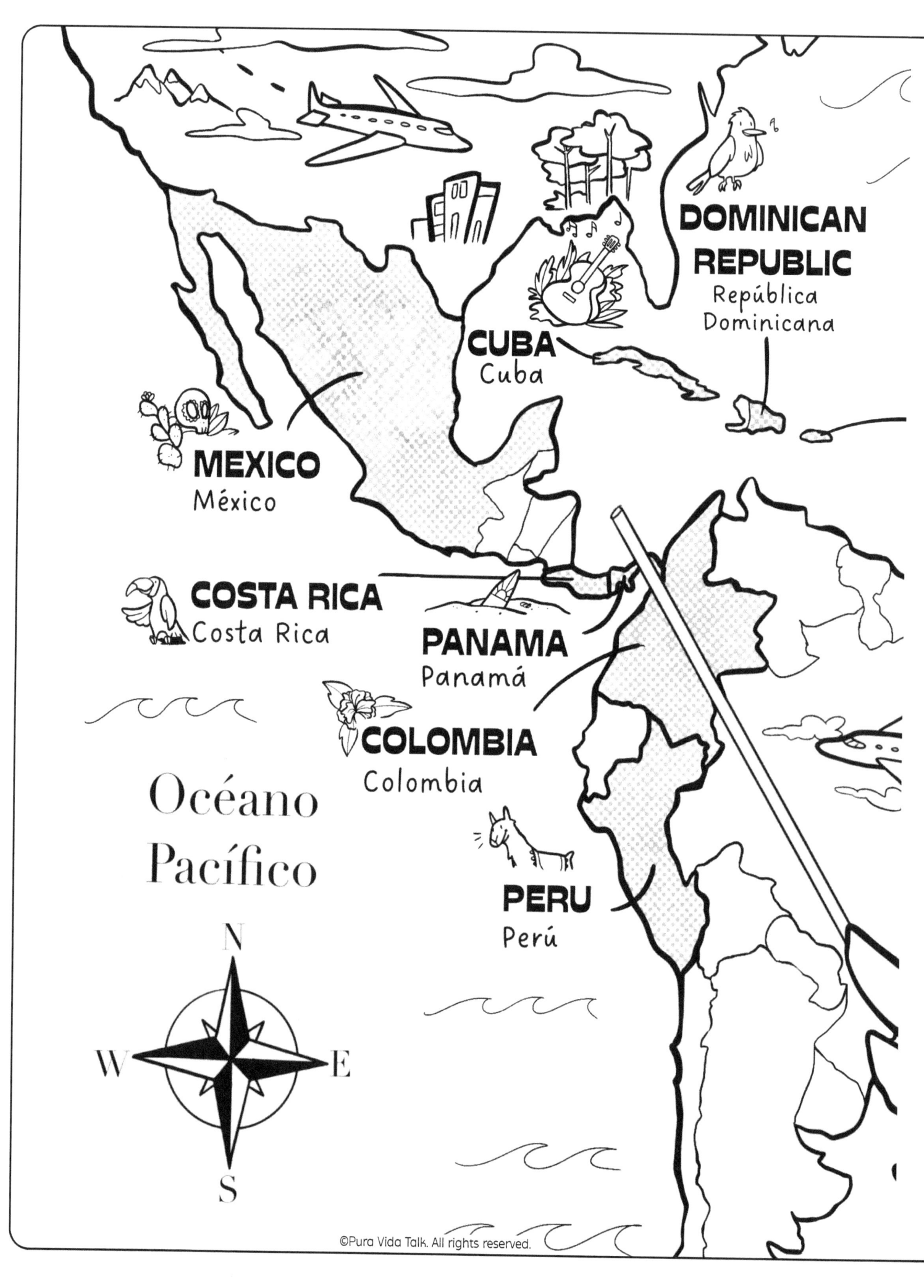

DOMINICAN REPUBLIC
República Dominicana

CUBA
Cuba

MEXICO
México

COSTA RICA
Costa Rica

PANAMA
Panamá

COLOMBIA
Colombia

Océano
Pacífico

PERU
Perú

N
W
E
S

©Pura Vida Talk. All rights reserved.

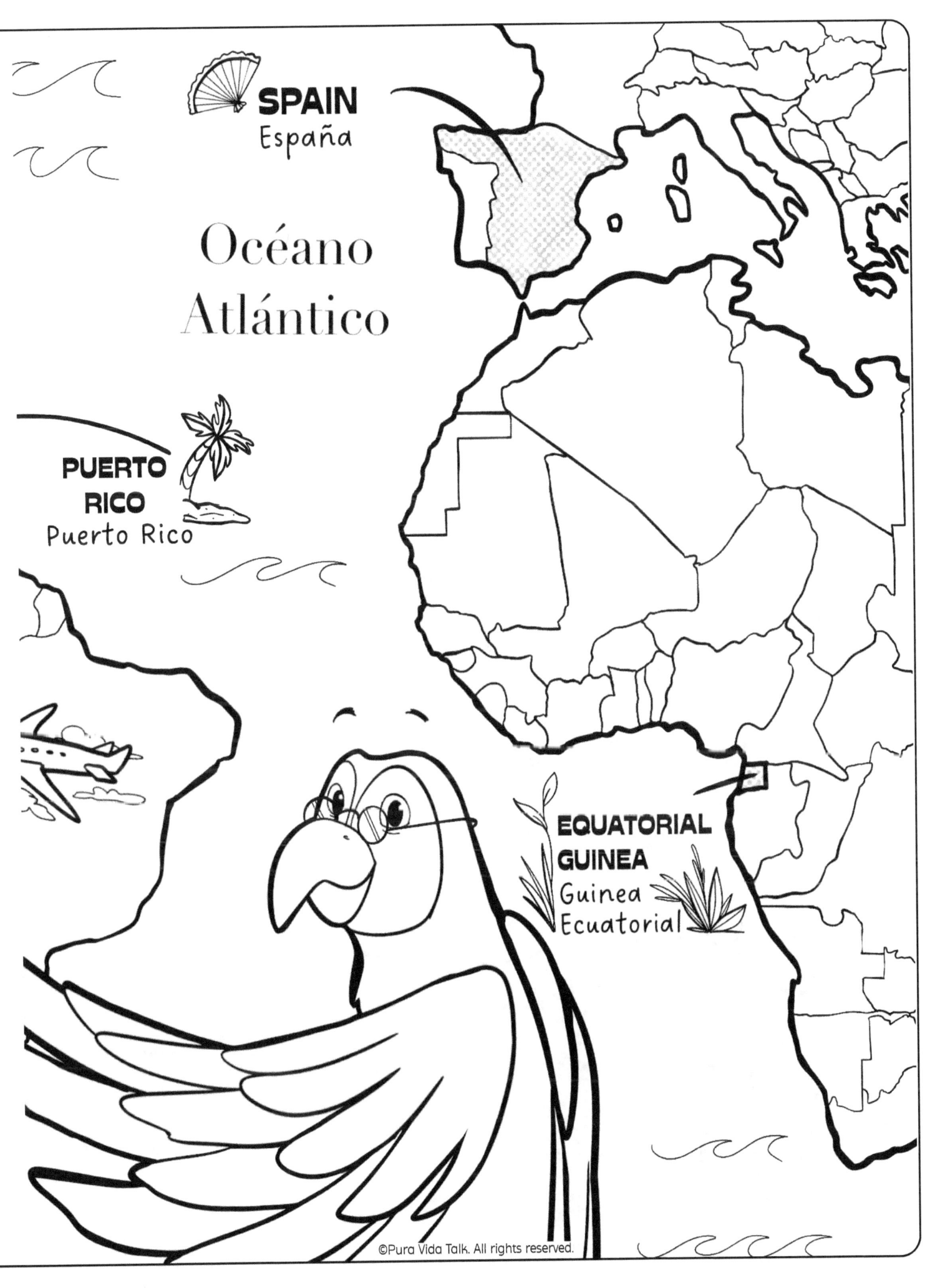

SPAIN
España

Océano
Atlántico

**PUERTO
RICO**
Puerto Rico

**EQUATORIAL
GUINEA**
Guinea
Ecuatorial

©Pura Vida Talk. All rights reserved.

©Pura Vida Talk. All rights reserved.

LET'S GET CRAFTING!

Hagamos manualidades

For this flag banner you will need...
Para esta actividad de banderas necesitarás...

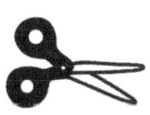
Scissors/Tijeras

Hole puncher/Perforador

Yarn/Hilo

Instructions

1 Find the flags throughout the book.
2 Cut along the marked lines.
3 Take the hole puncher and make 2 holes near the top.
4 Cut a length of string to the desired length of your banner and thread the string through each flag.
5 Once all the flags are on the string, tie the ends of the string to a sturdy object to display your authentic Hispanic flag banner.

Instrucciones

1 Encuentra las banderas dentro del libro.
2 Corta siguiendo las líneas marcadas.
3 Toma la perforadora y haz dos agujeros cerca de la parte superior.
4 Corta un trozo de hilo del largo deseado para tu banderín. Enhebra el hilo a través de cada banderín.
5 Una vez que todas las banderas estén en el hilo, ata los extremos del hilo a un objeto resistente para exhibir tu auténtica manualidad de banderas hispanas.

©Pura Vida Talk. All rights reserved.

LET'S GET CRAFTING!

Hagamos manualidades

For this latin art craft you will need...
Para esta manualidad de arte latino necesitarás...

Scissors/Tijeras

4 Photo frames/4 Marcos para fotos
x4

Instructions

1 Find the artwork throughout the book.
2 Cut along the marked lines.
3 Place the paper into the photo frame.
4 Secure the back of the photo frame and your art coloring craft is complete!

Instrucciones

1 Encuentra las obras de arte dentro del libro.
2 Corta siguiendo las líneas marcadas.
3 Coloca el papel en el marco de fotos.
4 ¡Asegura la parte posterior del marco y tu arte estará listo!

Latin artwork

Obras de arte latinas

©Pura Vida Talk. All rights reserved.

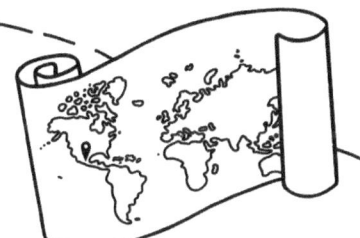

NORTH AMERICA
América del Norte

MEXICO
México

2

3

1

1 Red/Rojo

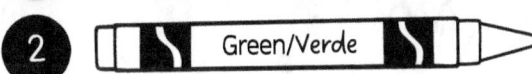
2 Green/Verde

3 White/Blanco

NOPAL

©Pura Vida Talk. All rights reserved.

©Pura Vida Talk. All rights reserved.

Alebrije

©Pura Vida Talk. All rights reserved.

Draw your own *alebrije*.
Dibuja tu propio *alebrije*.

Alebrijes are magical creatures that come from Mexican folk art.
Los *alebrijes* son criaturas mágicas que provienen del arte popular mexicano.

©Pura Vida Talk. All rights reserved.

Celebrating the Day of the Dead

Celebrando el Día de los Muertos

©Pura Vida Talk. All rights reserved.

©Pura Vida Talk. All rights reserved.

CARIBBEAN
Caribe

CUBA
Cuba

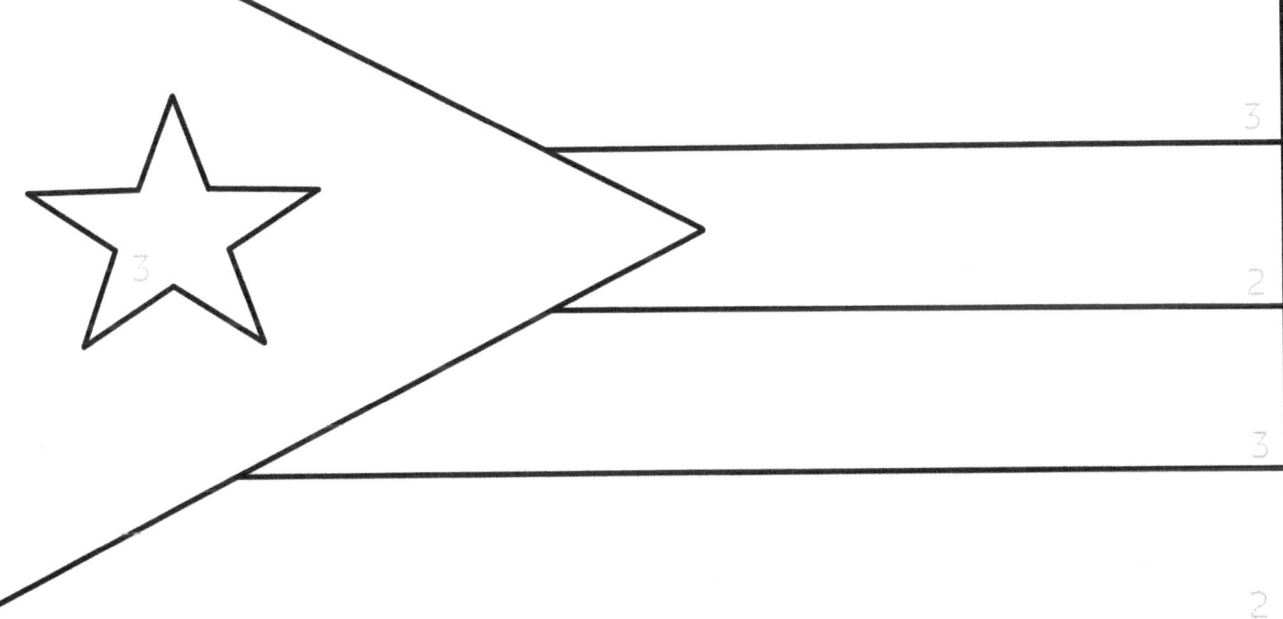

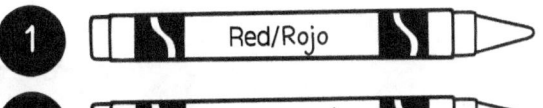

1 Red/Rojo

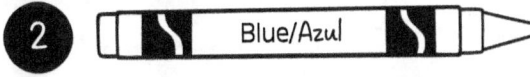

2 Blue/Azul

3 White/Blanco

Tocororo

©Pura Vida Talk. All rights reserved.

HAVANA

©Pura Vida Talk. All rights reserved.

The Capitol

El Capitolio

©Pura Vida Talk. All rights reserved.

"Cafecito"

©Pura Vida Talk. All rights reserved.

Salsa nights
Noches de salsa

©Pura Vida Talk. All rights reserved.

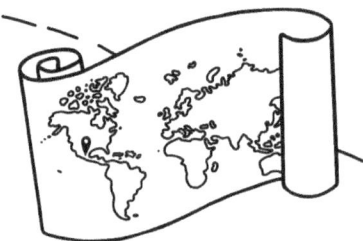

CARIBBEAN
Caribe

PUERTO RICO
Puerto Rico

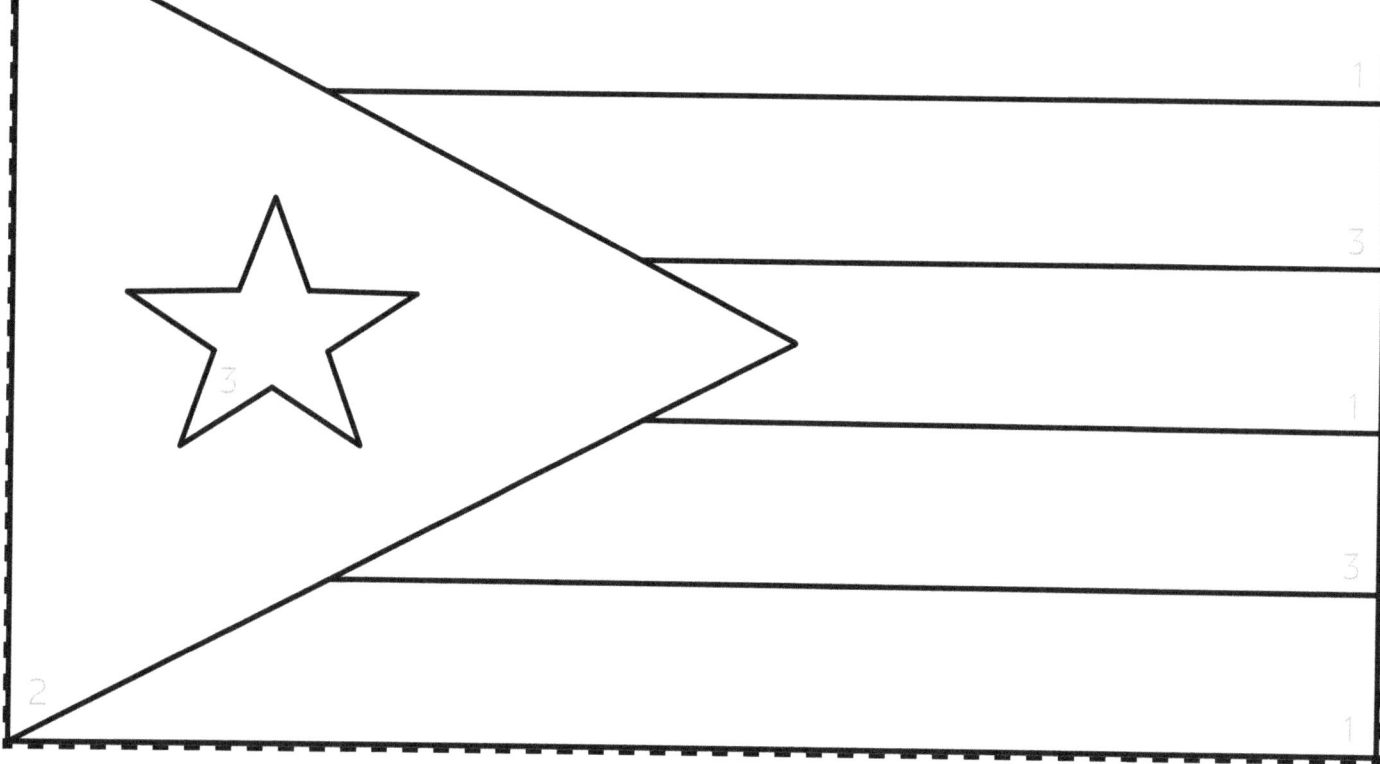

1	Red/Rojo
2	Blue/Azul
3	White/Blanco

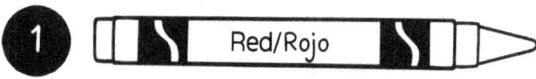
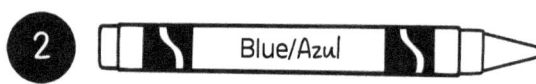

©Pura Vida Talk. All rights reserved.

GUESS THE FLAG

Adivina la bandera

1. Red/Rojo
2. Blue/Azul
3. White/Blanco

A

B

Could you tell which one is the Cuba flag and which one is the Puerto Rico flag?

¿Pudiste reconocer cuál es la bandera de Cuba y cuál es la bandera de Puerto Rico?

A. Puerto Rico   B. Cuba

©Pura Vida Talk. All rights reserved.

"La Isla"

AGUADILLA
Aguadilla

UTUADO
Utuado

CATHEDRAL OF SAINT
JOHN THE BAPTIST
Catedral San
Juan Bautista

FARO LOS MORRILLOS
Faro Los Morillos

MANATÍ
Manatí

SAN FELIPE DEL MORRO CASTLE
Castillo San Felipe del Morro

SALINAS
Salinas

El YUNQUE NATIONAL
FOREST
Bosque Nacional
EL Yunque

CULEBRA
ISLAND
Isla
Culebra

VIEQUE ISLAND
Isla Vieque

Puerto Rico

©Pura Vida Talk. All rights reserved.

Taínos
Gente buena
Good people

©Pura Vida Talk. All rights reserved.

©Pura Vida Talk. All rights reserved.

Sol Taíno

©Pura Vida Talk. All rights reserved.

Draw your own symbols!
¡Dibuja tus propios símbolos!

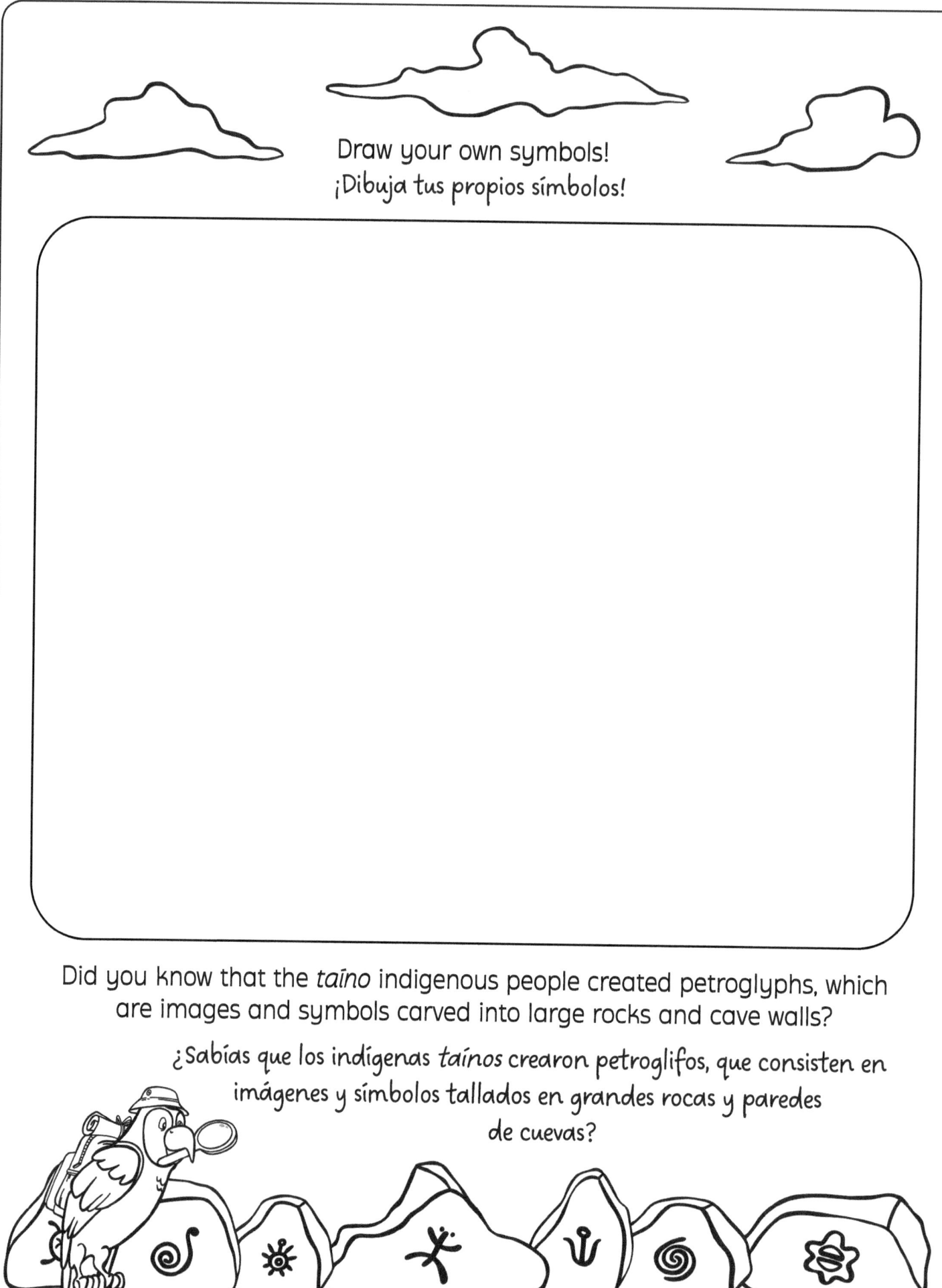

Did you know that the *taíno* indigenous people created petroglyphs, which are images and symbols carved into large rocks and cave walls?

¿Sabías que los indígenas *taínos* crearon petroglifos, que consisten en imágenes y símbolos tallados en grandes rocas y paredes de cuevas?

©Pura Vida Talk. All rights reserved.

SECRET MESSAGE

Mensaje secreto

Use the symbols to unlock the message!

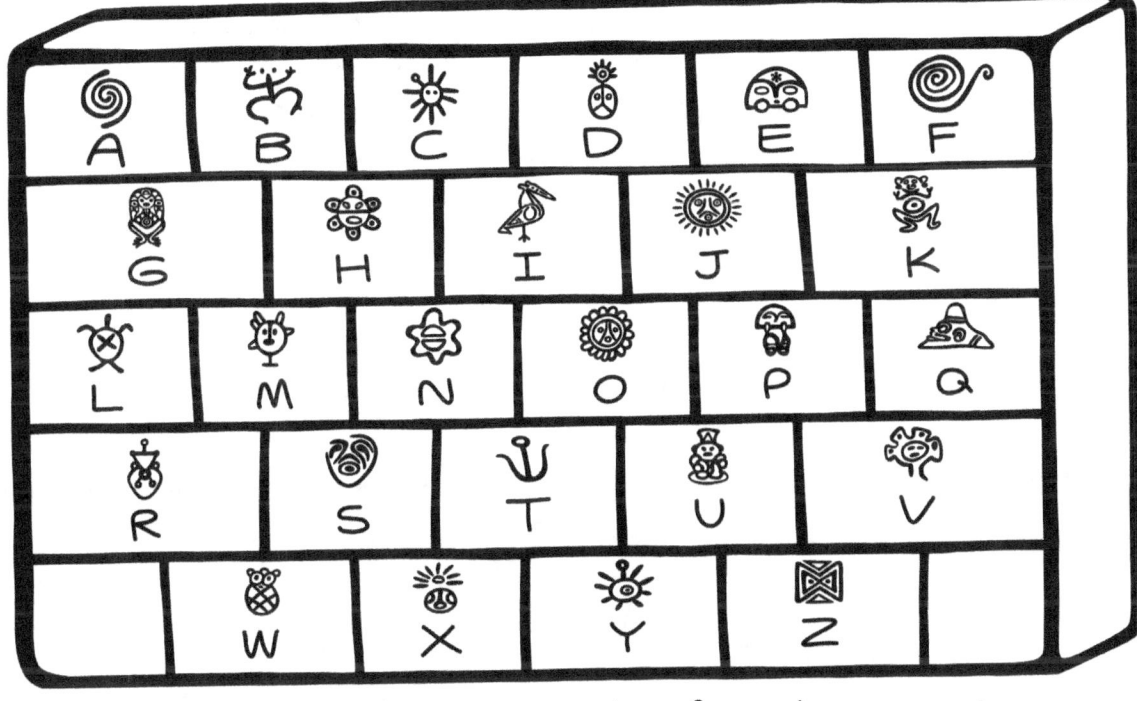

¡Usa los símbolos para descifrar el mensaje!

Did you unlock it? Find the answer below!

¿Lo lograste? ¡Encuentra la repuesta debajo!

The secret message is:
El mensaje secreto es:
La isla del Encanto
©Pura Vida Talk. All rights reserved.

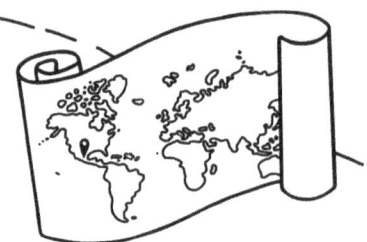

CARIBBEAN
Caribe

DOMINICAN REPUBLIC
República Dominicana

1	Red/Rojo
2	Blue/Azul
3	White/Blanco

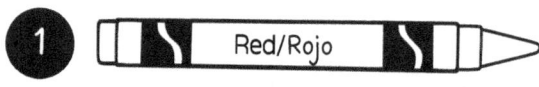
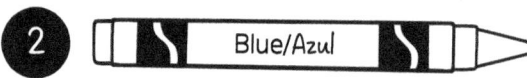
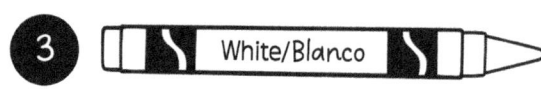

©Pura Vida Talk. All rights reserved.

Magical masks

Máscaras mágicas

©Pura Vida Talk. All rights reserved.

Happy merengue dance
Feliz baile de merengue

©Pura Vida Talk. All rights reserved.

Learn the names of these birds native to the Dominican Republic!
¡Aprende los nombres de estas aves nativas de la República Dominicana!

©Pura Vida Talk. All rights reserved.

1. Black-crowned tanager/Cuatro ojos coroninegro

2. Gray kingbird/Tirano dominicano

3. Scarlet macaw/Guacamayo macao

4. Broad-billed tody/Barrancolí picogrueso

5. Black-billed cuckoo/Cuclillo piquinegro

6. Hispaniolan spindalis/Cigua amarilla

7. Palmchat/Cigua palmera

8. Hispaniolan lizard cuckoo/Cuco lagartero de La Española

9. Magnificent frigatebird/Fragata real

HELP THE PALMCHAT

Ayuda a la cigua palmera

Choose the right path to help the palmchat reach her eggs!

¡Escoge el camino correcto para ayudar a la cigua palmera a alcanzar a sus huevos!

The correct path is: Ⓐ
El camino correcto es: Ⓐ

©Pura Vida Talk. All rights reserved.

CENTRAL AMERICA
América Central

COSTA RICA
Costa Rica

	2
	3
	1
	3
	2

1 Red/Rojo

2 Blue/Azul

3 White/Blanco

Volcán Arenal

©Pura Vida Talk. All rights reserved.

LA PAZ
WATERFALL
-CATARATA-

©Pura Vida Talk. All rights reserved.

©Pura Vida Talk. All rights reserved.

Pura

©Pura Vida Talk. All rights reserved.

Vida

©Pura Vida Talk. All rights reserved.

CENTRAL AMERICA
América Central

PANAMA
Panamá

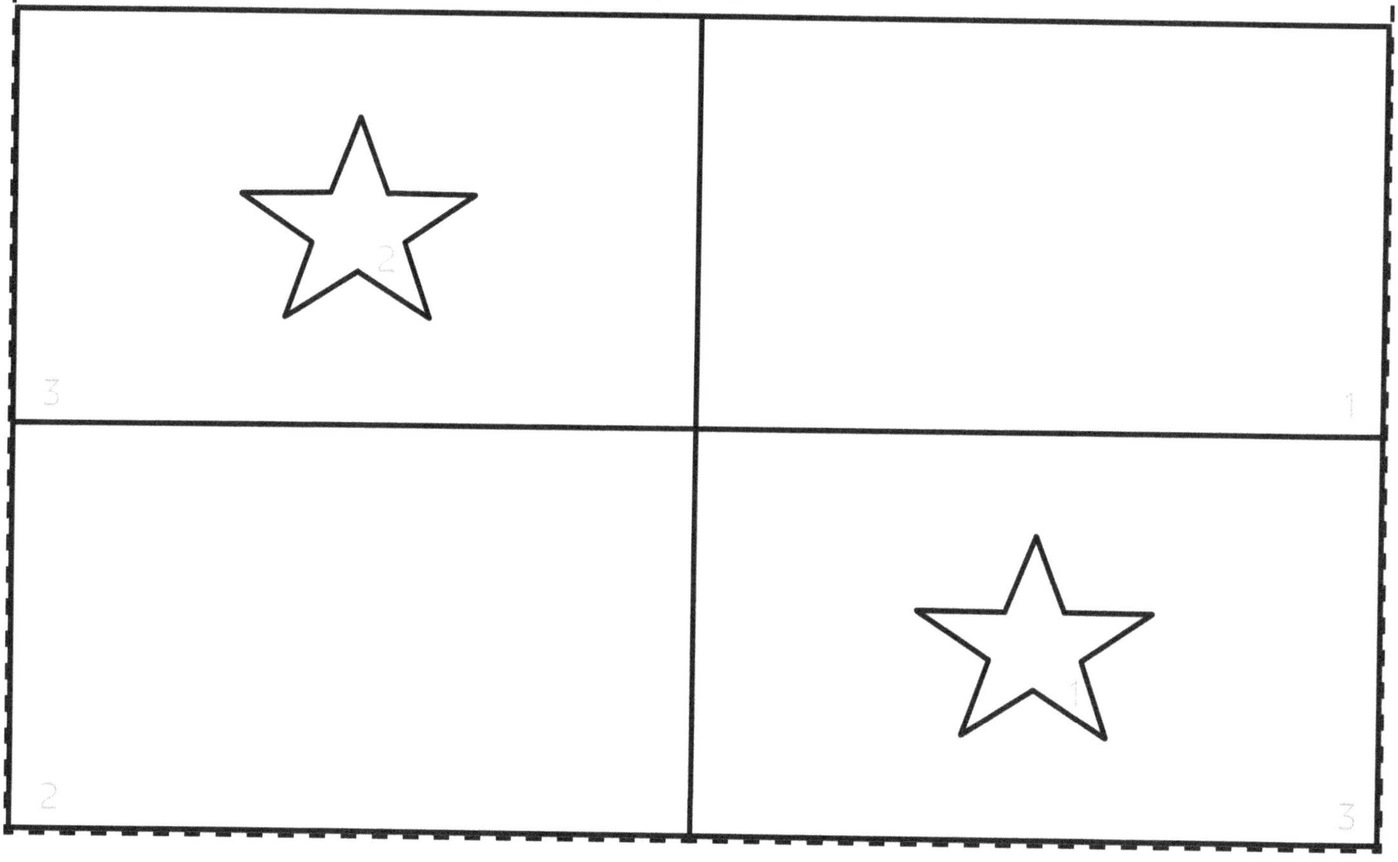

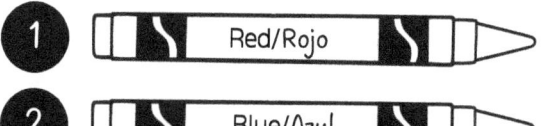
1 Red/Rojo

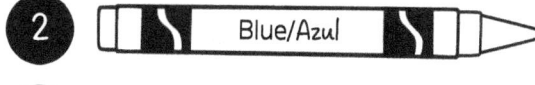
2 Blue/Azul

3 White/Blanco

Flor del Espíritu Santo

©Pura Vida Talk. All rights reserved.

Mola

©Pura Vida Talk. All rights reserved.

Draw your own *mola*!
¡Dibuja tu propia *mola*!

Did you know that the *mola* is a textile design made by the Guna indigenous of Panama?

¿Sabías que la *mola* es un diseño textil hecho por los indígenas Gunas de Panamá?

©Pura Vida Talk. All rights reserved.

DOT-TO-DOT

Conecta los puntos

Connect the dots to reveal the panamanian golden frog!

¡Conecta los puntos para revelar la rana dorada panameña!

©Pura Vida Talk. All rights reserved.

ECO-CROSSWORD

Eco-crucigrama

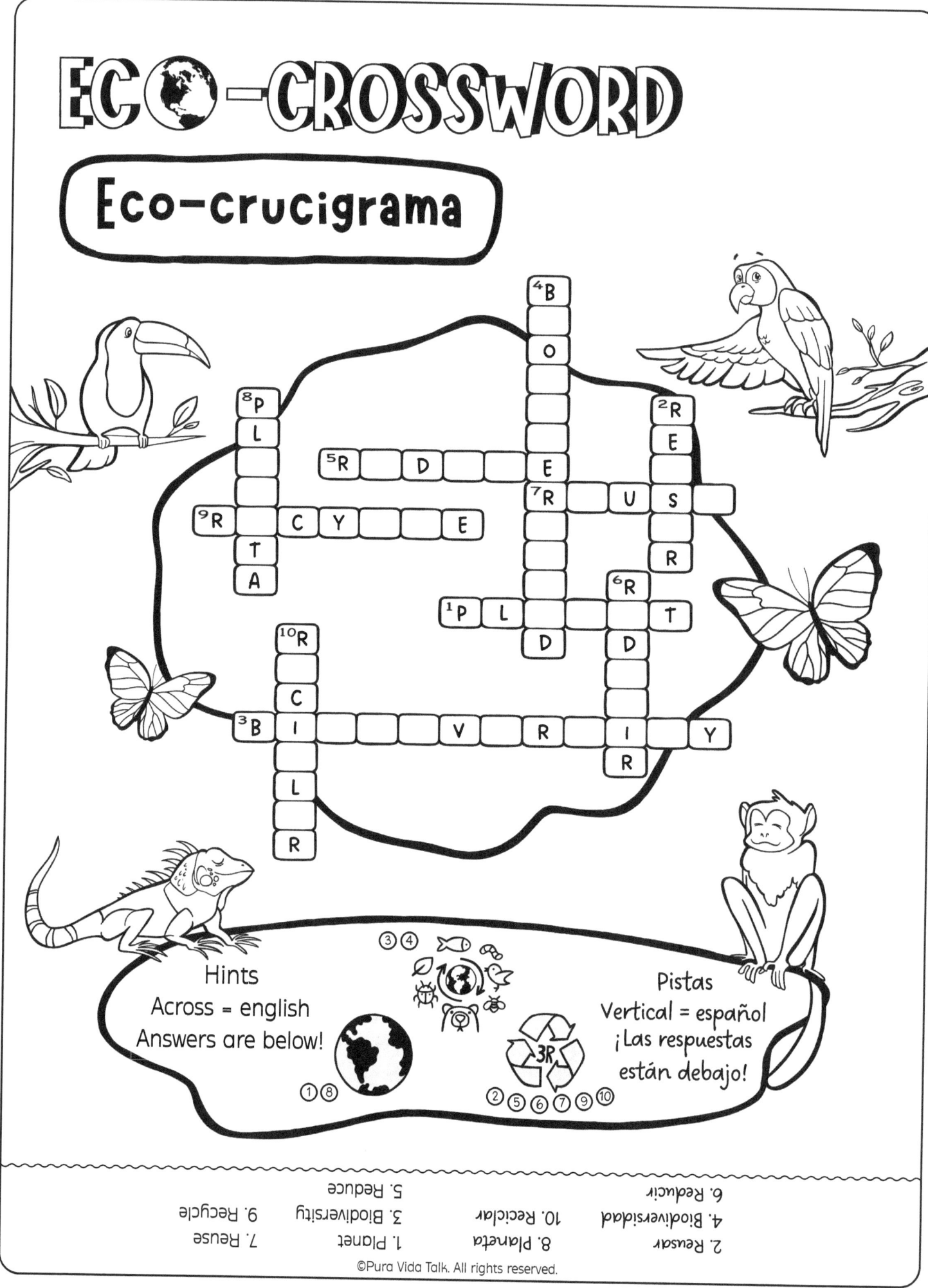

Hints
Across = english
Answers are below!

Pistas
Vertical = español
¡Las respuestas están debajo!

5. Reduce
3. Biodiversity
9. Recycle
1. Planet
10. Reciclar
8. Planeta
6. Reducir
4. Biodiversidad
2. Reusar
7. Reuse

©Pura Vida Talk. All rights reserved.

Panama City
Ciudad de Panamá

©Pura Vida Talk. All rights reserved.

The Panama Canal
El Canal de Panamá

©Pura Vida Talk. All rights reserved.

©Pura Vida Talk. All rights reserved

CANAL MAZE

Laberinto del canal

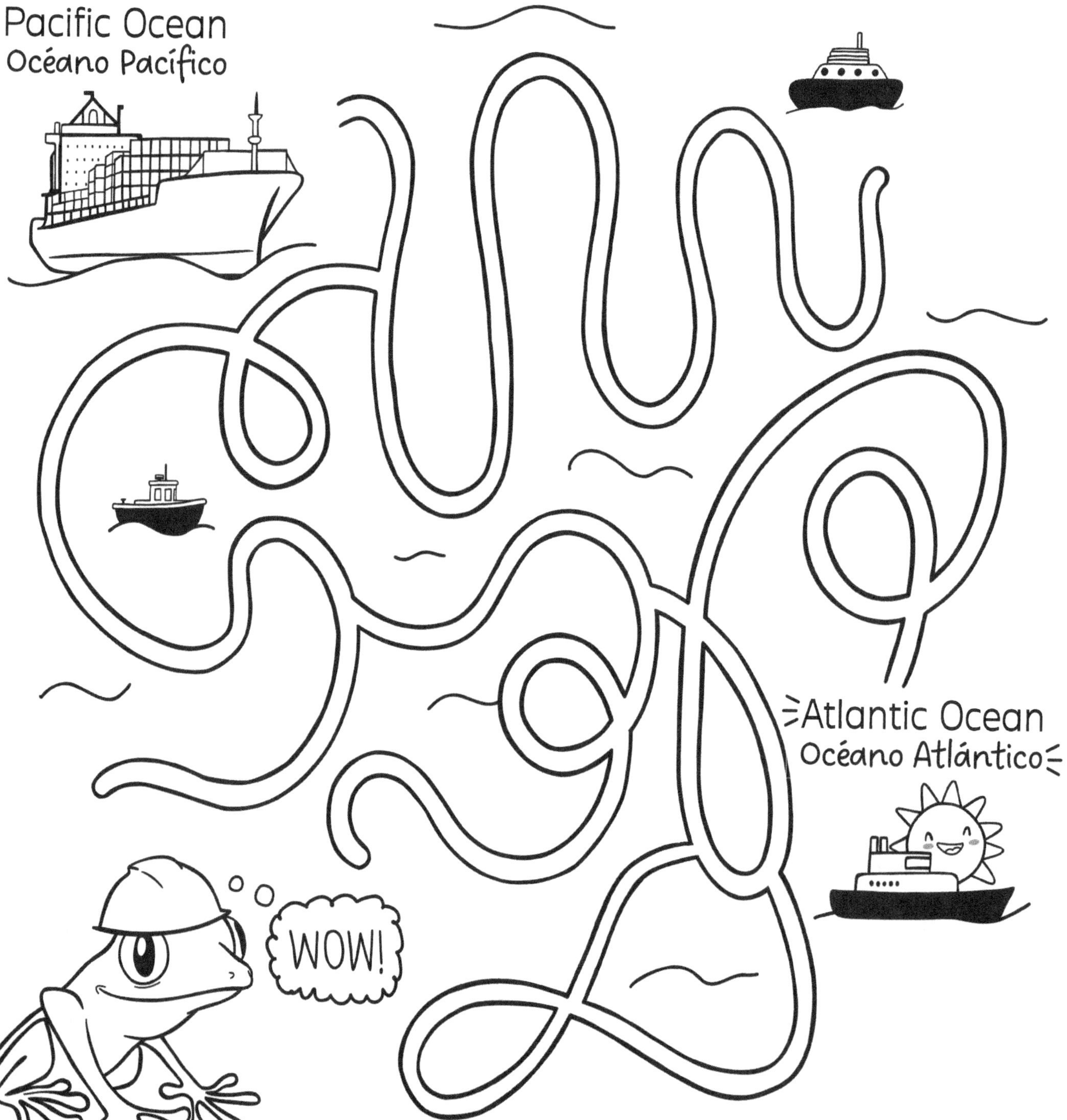

Pacific Ocean
Océano Pacífico

Atlantic Ocean
Océano Atlántico

WOW!

©Pura Vida Talk. All rights reserved.

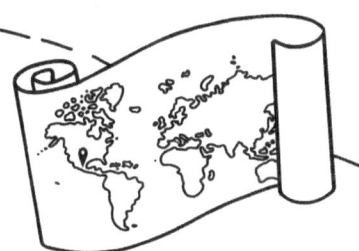

SOUTH AMERICA
América del Sur

COLOMBIA
Colombia

3

2

1

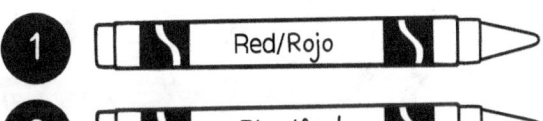
1 — Red/Rojo

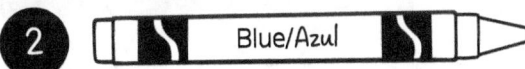
2 — Blue/Azul

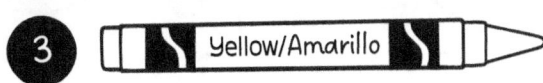
3 — Yellow/Amarillo

GUATAPÉ

©Pura Vida Talk. All rights reserved.

COCORA
Colombia

©Pura Vida Talk. All rights reserved.

Palenquera

©Pura Vida Talk. All rights reserved.

Can you draw your favorite fruits?
¿Puedes dibujar tus frutas preferidas?

Did you know *palanqueras* are colorful fruit sellers?
¿Sabías que las palanqueras son vendedoras de fruta vestidas con trajes coloridos?

©Pura Vida Talk. All rights reserved.

Colombian petals

Pétalos colombianos

©Pura Vida Talk. All rights reserved.

UNSCRAMBLE

Descifra la palabra

1 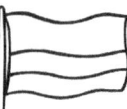 B I A M C O L O | B I A M C O L O

2  L A N T P | A L A N T P

3  A L L E V A N T O | A L L E V A N T O

4  O R E S | A S O R

5  O F C E F E | A C É F

6  M A L P | A L P R A M E

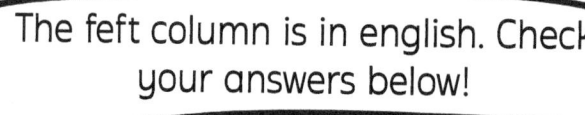

The feft column is in english. Check your answers below!

La columna derecha está en español. ¡Revisa tus respuestas debajo!

2. Plant   1. Colombia   2. Planta   1. Colombia
4. Rose   3. Vallenato   4. Rosa   3. Vallenato
6. Palm   5. Coffee   6. Palmera   5. Café

©Pura Vida Talk. All rights reserved.

Made in Colombia

Hecho en Colombia

©Pura Vida Talk. All rights reserved.

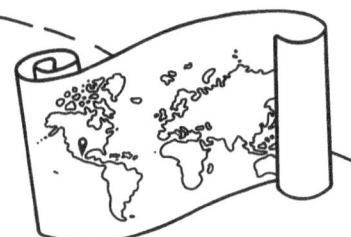

SOUTH AMERICA
América del Sur

PERU
Perú

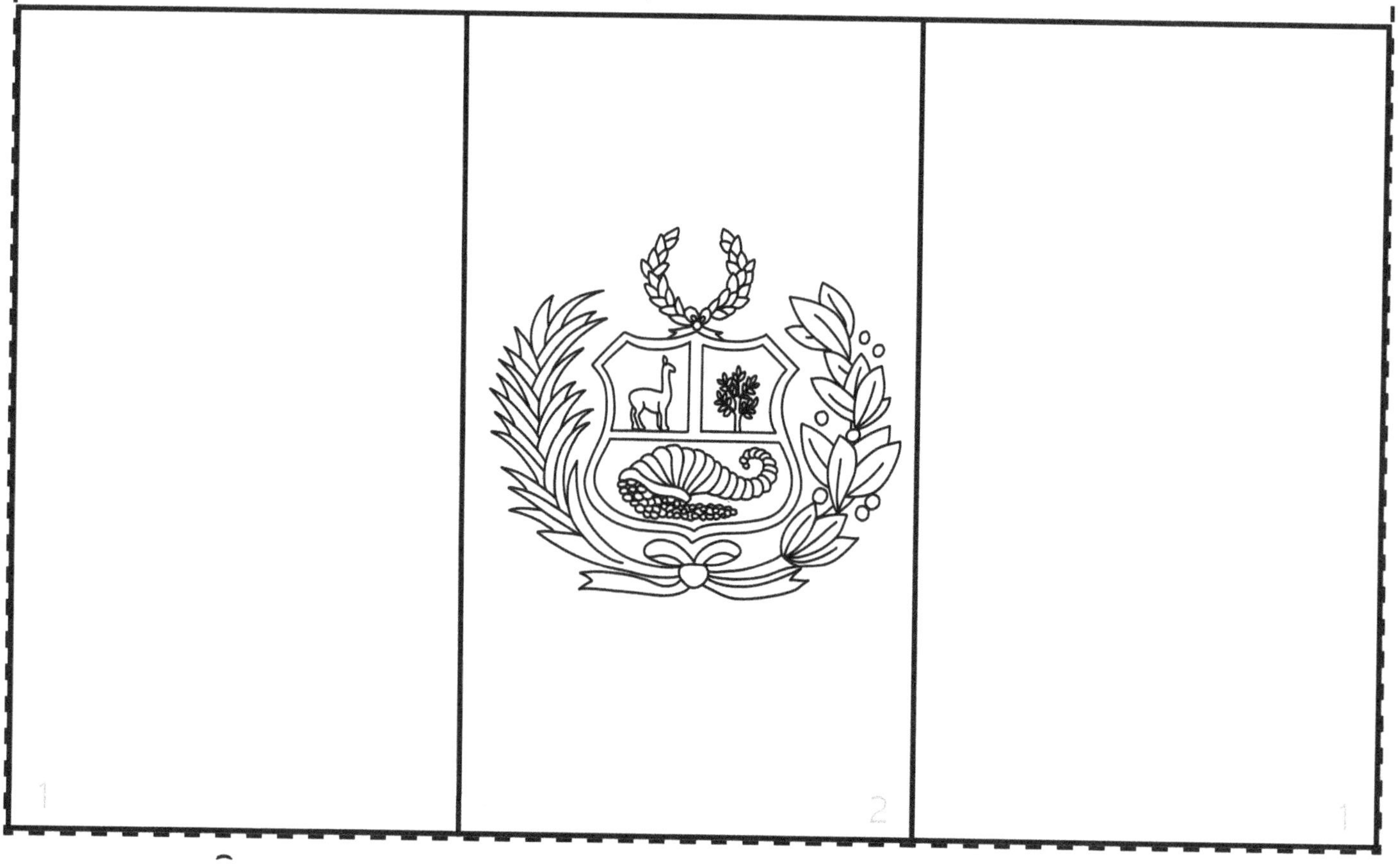

1 — Red/Rojo

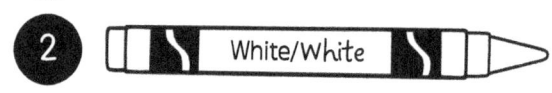
2 — White/White

Vinicunca
CUSCO

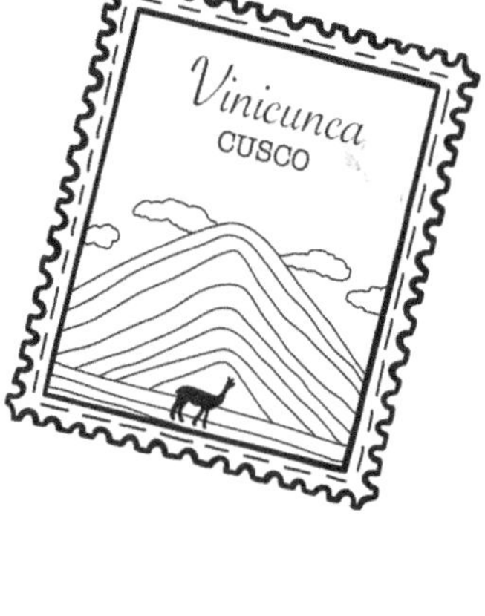

©Pura Vida Talk. All rights reserved.

©Pura Vida Talk. All rights reserved.

Friends in Vinicunca

Amigos en Vinicunca

©Pura Vida Talk. All rights reserved.

Learn spanish: Discover a superpower!

Aprende español: ¡Descubre un superpoder!

600 million

millones

speakers

de hablantes

©Pura Vida Talk. All rights reserved.

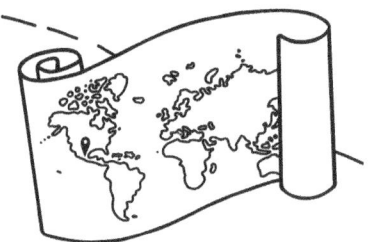

EUROPE
Europa

✂

SPAIN
España

1 Red/Rojo

2 Yellow/Amarillo

BARCELONA

©Pura Vida Talk. All rights reserved.

Flamenco

Flamenco

©Pura Vida Talk. All rights reserved.

©Pura Vida Talk. All rights reserved.

©Pura Vida Talk. All rights reserved.

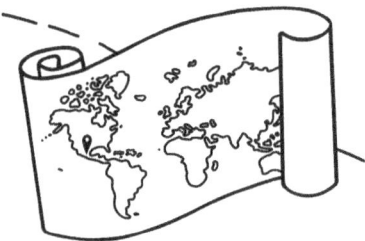

AFRICA
África

✂

EQUATORIAL GUINEA
Guinea Ecuatorial

1 — Red/Rojo

2 — White/Blanco

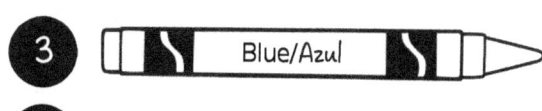
3 — Blue/Azul

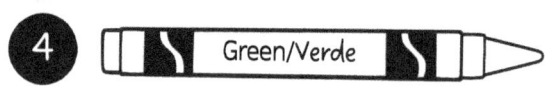
4 — Green/Verde

Parque Nacional Monte Alén

©Pura Vida Talk. All rights reserved.

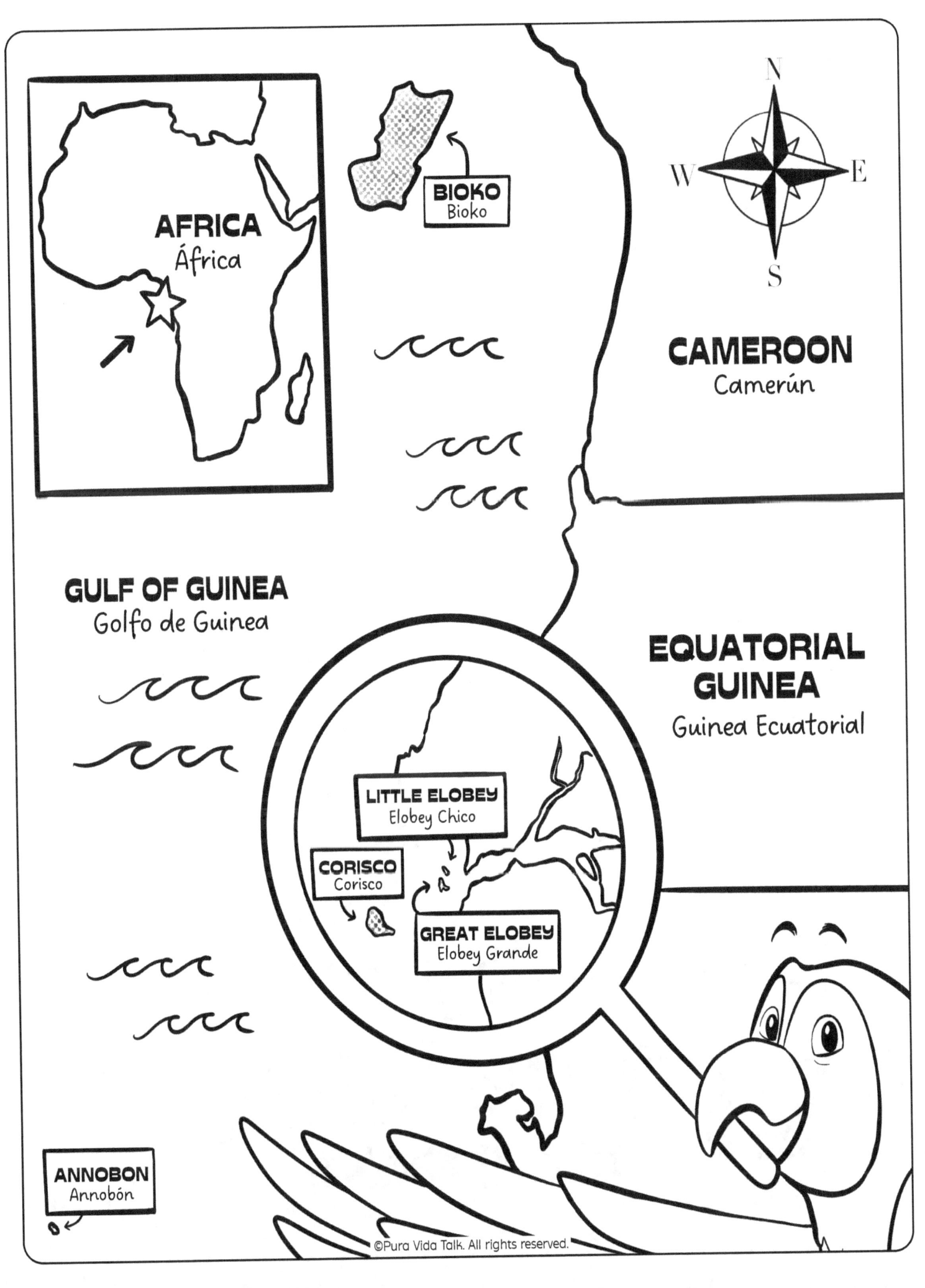

AFRICA
África

BIOKO
Bioko

CAMEROON
Camerún

N
W E
S

GULF OF GUINEA
Golfo de Guinea

EQUATORIAL
GUINEA
Guinea Ecuatorial

LITTLE ELOBEY
Elobey Chico

CORISCO
Corisco

GREAT ELOBEY
Elobey Grande

ANNOBON
Annobón

©Pura Vida Talk. All rights reserved.

Bioko drill
El dril Bioko

©Pura Vida Talk. All rights reserved.

Equatorial Guinea fauna

Fauna de Guinea Ecutorial

©Pura Vida Talk. All rights reserved.

MUSIC WORD SEARCH

Sopa de letras musical

```
Y K Q I Z A E U O H N G F Z R
X E W V N C N B O C U M B I A
N L Q J H A I V L M O U L M R
E A G B R L N G X J Z A Y A E
C F X X G I V Q I I V H Y R G
W C S R K P A T A S T D M I G
Q G E Y H S L H H V V V T A A
R A V U P O L E S M G E P C E
M B Z J Z T E K D F S J G H T
H O T O T L N V U S X F F I O
W M N E Y U A Q O O W M S O N
Z B I M X B T M E R E N G U E
M A K R S F O M A M B O B N E
H H S C B W Z K J X A V B X E
E S A L S A B Y U C X K P V O
```

Find and circle the music related words!

Salsa	Merengue	Calipso
Mambo	Reggaeton	Cumbia
Bomba	Mariachi	Vallenato

¡Encuentra y encierra en un círculo las
palabras musicales!

©Pura Vida Talk. All rights reserved.

Hispanic colors
celebrating diversity
Colores hispanos: Celebrando la diversidad

©Pura Vida Talk. All rights reserved.

©Pura Vida Talk. All rights reserved.

www.ingramcontent.com/pod-product-compliance
Lightning Source LLC
Chambersburg PA
CBHW080855120626
46553CB00009B/2632